# 卐 Indian 卐 Mythology Story Book for Kids

# Ganesha Stories

## Lakhi Cholan

# CHAPTER 1

# The Story of
# Lord Ganesha's Birth

# Lord Shiva and Goddess Parvati lived on Mount Kailash.

Most of the time, Lord Shiva would be out fulfilling other important duties which left Goddess Parvati alone in the mountains...

Goddess Parvati created the statue of a child from turmeric and breathed life into him.

A boy was born and Goddess Parvati accepted him as her son by naming him 'Ganesha'.

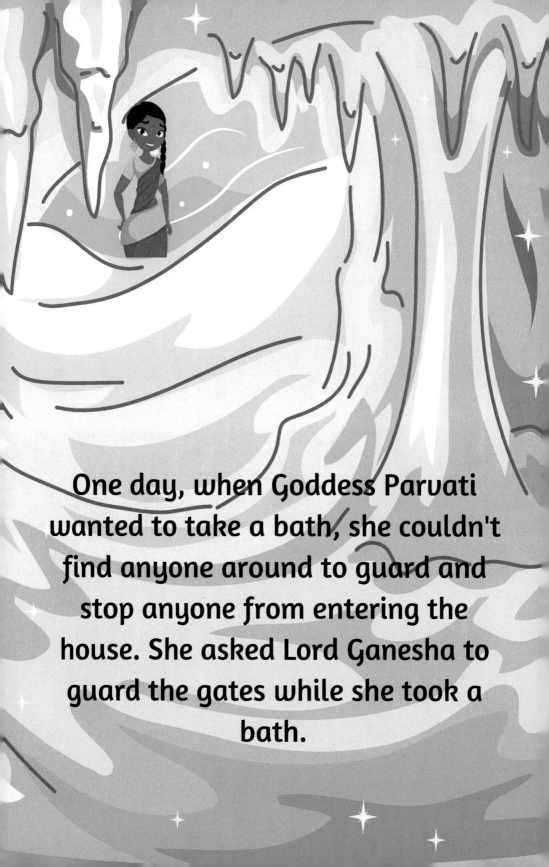

One day, when Goddess Parvati wanted to take a bath, she couldn't find anyone around to guard and stop anyone from entering the house. She asked Lord Ganesha to guard the gates while she took a bath.

At that time, Lord Shiva came home and proceeded towards the gates..

Lord Shiva was not aware of the child's birth by Goddess Parvati, so he was furious when Lord Ganesh did not allow him inside his house. So he sent his forces to scare the child away. But Ganesha had the special powers which was bestowed upon him by Goddess Parvati.

So, he defeated Lord Shiva's army very easily and laughed upon it. Also, he did not know that Lord Shiva was his father.

Lord Shiva was furious at the child's behaviour and lost his temper. He ended up beheading Lord Ganesha's Head in a fury.

When Goddess Parvati stepped out, she was shocked to see the headless body of her son, which made her extremely furious!

She yelled at Lord Shiva and vowed to destroy the entire world as a result of his actions.

Lord Brahma witnessed the events and appeared in front of Goddess Parvati. He prayed to her and asked her not to destroy the world. He asked for mercy for the innocent lives on the earth.

Goddess Parvati changed her mind on the condition that her son be brought back to life.

Lord Shiva was filled with guilt and realised his mistake. The boy's love towards his mother was exceptional. He agreed to bring the boy back to life, but the impact of the punishment from his trident was irreversible. So he had to find another solution

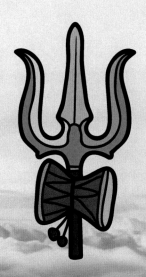

Nandi

He told his bull 'Nandi', to go to the forest and bring the head of the first animal who is found sleeping away from its mother.

Only a calf who did not love his mother would be away from her. By chance, they found an elephant calf sleeping away from its mother.

Nandi brought back the head of an elephant. Lord Shiva placed the elephant head over the body and brought him back to life.

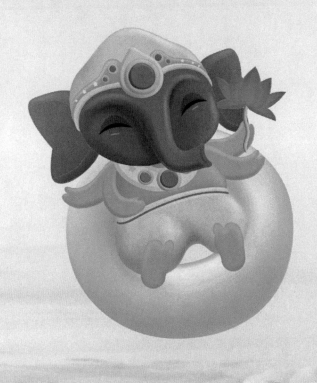

Goddess Parvati was rejoiced with her son's rejuvenation. But she felt sad that other would mock him for his unusual appearence.

Lord Shiva understood Goddess Parvati's fears and summoned all the gods. They blessed the boy with many supernatural powers and boons.

They named him 'Ganesha'. He is also known as 'Ganapati'.

The Gods and Goddesses also blessed him as the master of wisdom and intelligence. This is how he was born and known as the 'God of Gods'.

CHAPTER 2

# The Story of Lord Ganesha and Kubera

Lord Kubera was a eminent God who was admired for being the most wealthiest of all Gods in the entire universe.

He liked to showcase his wealth to everyone. On such occasion, he went to invite Lord Shiva and Goddess Parvati for a feast at his house Gold palace.

They understood his intention. So, they sent their son 'Lord Ganesh' instead of them. Kubera was triumphant as he believed that feeding Lord Ganesh wouldn't be a difficult as a child wouldn't eat that much.

Lord Ganesh went to Lord Kuber's house for the feast. However, he noticed his behaviour as too extravagant. Lord Ganesha understood that Lord Kuber was too proud about his riches. He wanted to teach him a lesson. So, he started devouring all the food and finished everything..

Kubera sent his workers to the nearby villages to get some food for Ganesha in order to avoid humiliation. Lord Shiva and Goddess Parvati's smart son had eaten everything that was given to him, but was still hungry. As Kubera was standing helplessly, he asked for more food.

He barely left any food for the guests. He asked Lord Kuber, "I want more food. bring me more."

Lord Kuber was scared and said "Its all over. Nothing is left now!"

Lord Ganesha replied angrily, "This is how you treat your guests? Bring me more food or else i will eat everything i find over here."

Lord Ganesha was so hungry that he started eating anything he could find in his vicinity.

Kubera cried out to Lord Shiva and Goddess Parvati for help in order to save himself from the insult of not being worthy of feeding a little child.

Lord Shiva was well aware of the royal crushing of Kubera's pride by their son Ganesha. So, he handed over a fistful of rice to Lord Kubera, and asked him to feed his son.

When he ate this small bowl of rice from Lord Kubera, Lord Ganesha was pleased with his hunger.

Ganesha therefore made Kubera realize that no wealth would fulfill one's hunger if it is offered with false pride or ego. He could have received the blessings of all, had he arranged the feast to feed people out of kindness, love and respect.

CHAPTER 3

# Lord Ganesha and the Moon

Once upon a time, there was a huge feast, inviting many gods and goddesses. The party was also attended by Lord Ganesha. They prepared many special sweets and dishes which were his favorites to make him feel special and prove their devotion to Lord Ganesha.

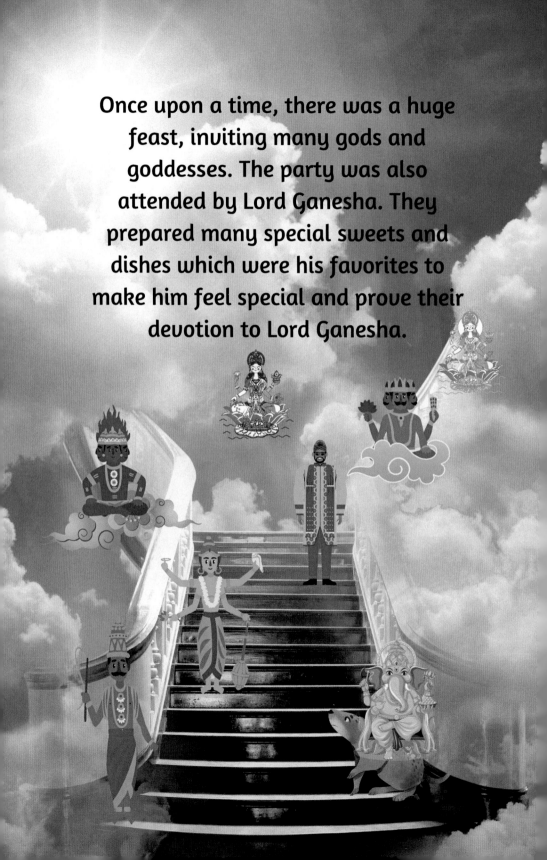

As we all know, Lord Ganesha was very fond of eating food. So, he used to eat until everything was finished. He didn't want anyone to notice this.

After the feast was over, he waited until night and left when nobody could see him. He also took some of his favourite sweets for the journey.

While he was going home,
some of his sweets fell down
and he bent down to pick them.

Suddenly, Lord Ganesha heard
someone laughing loudly.

You will be
invisible
forever!

Lord Ganesha felt embarressed and
looked around. When he lifted up
his head he saw the moon laughing
at him. He got enraged and
immediately cursed the moon that
it will be invisible forever.

The moon was saddened when he
heard it and asked Lord Ganesha
for forgiveness. Lord Ganesha was
also guily that he cursed the moon
without thinking about it.

He tried to pardon him, but it could not be taken back when a curse is imposed. Thus Lord Ganesha came up with a way of reducing the curse.

He announced that each day the moon will become smaller and remain invisible for one day in a month, which we call as 'Amavasya' and regard it as inauspicious.

We should be kind in our
actions and forgive those
who repent their mistakes.

# CHAPTER 4
# The Story of The Missing Conch

Lord Vishnu was known to carry around
his favourite conch with him at all times.
One fine day, he noticed that his
favourite conch was missing.

He was very displeased at this and
searched all around the world for his
favourite conch.

As Lord Vishnu was on the search for his conch, he heard the loud sound coming from his conch from far away. He immediately followed the sound and landed on Mount Kailash to find Lord Ganesha having fun blowing the conch.

Lord Vishnu knew that it won't be easy to convince Lord Ganesha. So, he asked Lord Shiva for his help. Lord Shiva said that Lord Ganesha found the conch lying around and he did not have the power to convince him to return it. However, he suggested Lord Vishnu to perform a puja for Lord Ganesha to appease him.

Lord Vishnu did puja for Lord Ganesha with full devotion. Lord Ganesha was immensely pleased and understood that he was holding Lord Vishnu's conch.

Lord Ganesha gave the conch back
to Lord Vishnu without hesitation.

This story teaches us modesty,
patience and compassion.

# CHAPTER 5

# The Story of
# The Bowl of Sweet Kheer

Once upon a time, Lord Ganesha entered a village in a form of a brahmin boy holding a bag of rice in one hand and a bottle of milk on the other.

He asked each and every one for help in making Kheer, but everyone were busy.

On the way, he reached a poor woman's hut who was busy with her work. But she agreed to help him in making the sweet kheer for him.

She was already feeling tired due to working in the farm. But she didn't hesitate to help the boy. As she mixed the rice and milk in the pot, she fell asleep due to tiredness

When she woke up the boy was nowhere to be found as he was playing outside in the fields.

The boy answered that when she gave the bowl to the Ganesha photo, he had eaten it too. The woman started to weep and realised that it was Lord Ganesha. He blessed her with good health, wealth and long life.

Visit us at

www.srichants.com

# Citations

The Story Of Lord Ganesha's Birth - SriChants. (2021, December 17). SriChants. https://srichants.com/the-story-of-lord-ganeshas-birth/

https://en.wikipedia.org/wiki/Ganesha

## Book Cover credits:
"vectorpouch/Shutterstock.com"
Item ID: 1052574872

As per the **CREDIT AND COPYRIGHT NOTICES** of shutterstock.com, an adjacent credit to the Shutterstock contributor and to Shutterstock is clearly mentioned above in correct size, color and prominence in a clear and easily readable manner.
Please refer: https://www.shutterstock.com/license

All other Images/Graphics/Vectors used from Canva comes under 'Free Media License Agreement' where under **"Permitted Uses"** of **Canva designs** that contain Free Stock Media. clearly states that 'All free Photos, Music, Graphics, Images and Video files on Canva can be used for free for commercial and noncommercial use'.
Please refer: https://www.canva.com/policies/free-media/

One or more images used on the Book cover comes under the "Permitted uses" of Canva Designs. This book was created using 'Canva Pro'. The author of this Book has the right to include all images in this book (ebook/Paperback).

For permissions contact:
srichants@gmail.com

Srichants offers Vedic Astrology - Horoscope Services to get solutions and remedies for your life. Srichants.com is one of the world's Best Astrology Website run by a team of trustworthy and reliable Chief Astrologers.

Visit us @ www.srichants.com

1. VEDIC CHANTS - ANCIENT HEALING MANTRAS & HYMNS
2. VEDIC ASTROLOGY HOROSCOPE SERVICES
3. CUSTOMIZED MANTRAS/PUJA RITUALS FOR FESTIVALS
4. EXPERT REMEDIES FOR LIFE PROBLEMS BY CHIEF ASTROLOGERS
5. FREE MANTRAS IN PDF FORMAT FOR NEW SUBSCRIBERS !!!

THANK YOU FOR YOUR CONTINUED SUPPORT!

For updates, follow our official website: www.srichants.com
Contact us: srichants@gmail.com

Made in the USA
Las Vegas, NV
09 September 2022